"THE 'TOO MUCH' that piques the reader's interest in the arresting title of these poems does double service: it sounds a cry of anguished exasperation uttered by this collection and comments on the way private life has been massively invaded by public upheavals. A startling theme, viewed with unexpected ambivalence, is hope—or rather 'the carcass of hope'— that in these poems seems fated to end with 'passionate disappointment.' As the immigrant daughter of political exiles, I grasp that theme viscerally as Kalfopoulou pursues it through marvelous use of sensory details; attention to the voices and narratives of individuals, named and specified; love poems both tender and erotically vivid; memories of the dead; encounters with the maimed but still-living; physical vestiges of World War II and its victims, and travel accounts full of foreboding amid strangers in nocturnal surroundings."

—RHINA P. ESPAILLAT,
author of *Playing at Stillness* and *Her Place in These Designs*

A History of Too Much

of Too

Much

Adrianne Kalfopoulou

poems

 Red Hen Press | *Pasadena, CA*

Book design by Annie Dills
Cover art by INO

Library of Congress Cataloging-in-Publication Data
Names: Kalfopoulou, Adrianne, author.
Title: A history of too much / Adrianne Kalfopoulou.
Description: First edition. | Pasadena, CA : Red Hen Press, [2018]
Identifiers: LCCN 2017029206 | ISBN 9781597096126 (softcover : acid-free paper)
    ISBN 9781597097543 (ebook)
Classification: LCC PS3611.A4328 A6 2018 | DDC 811/.6—dc23
LC record available at https://lccn.loc.gov/2017029206

The National Endowment for the Arts, the Los Angeles County Arts Commission, the Ahmanson Foundation, the Dwight Stuart Youth Fund, the Max Factor Family Foundation, the Pasadena Tournament of Roses Foundation, the Pasadena Arts & Culture Commission and the City of Pasadena Cultural Affairs Division, the City of Los Angeles Department of Cultural Affairs, the Audrey & Sydney Irmas Charitable Foundation, the Kinder Morgan Foundation, the Allergan Foundation, the Riordan Foundation, and the Amazon Literary Partnership partially support Red Hen Press.

First Edition
Published by Red Hen Press
www.redhen.org

ACKNOWLEDGMENTS

My gratitude and thanks to the editors of these publications for publishing my work, sometimes in slightly different forms:

Bookforum: "Slowly" (in Greek, translated by Katerina Iliopoulou); *Calamaro*: "Xxx . . ."; *Duende*: "Poem in Pieces, a Log"; *Ergon, Greek/American Arts and Letters*: "The Goodbyes"; *Fogged Clarity*: "The History of Too Much"; *Futures*: Poetry of the Greek Crisis (Penned in the Margins, 2015): "A History of Too Much," "This City," "Those Days," and "Ungodly"; *Harvard Review Online*: "Coming down the Mountain before Dark"; *Journal of the Motherhood Initiative* (JMI): "First Audition"; *The Love Index* (Dancing Girl Press, 2017): "In a Pomegranate Time," "Lunar," "The Road," and "The Stranger Joy"; *Michigan Quarterly Review*: "Fatherland," "The Taxi Driver Laments"; *Nimrod International Journal*: "Sea"; *Soundings: A journal of politics and culture*: "This City" (reprint); *Taos Journal of International Poetry & Art*: "Reading with Ethel," and "Those Days"; *WORDPEACE*: "Because the News Was Bad"; *Valparaiso Poetry Review*: "Skin."

"A History of Too Much," "The Evening the Referendum Was Repealed," "The Startled Dreams of the Fallen in Spring," "This City," "Those Days," and "Ungodly" were included in *The Cultural Politics of the Greek Crisis*, a networking project at the University of Birmingham that is curated by Dimitris Tziovas (http://culpolgreekcrisis.com/2015/05/06/austeritys-city/).

To my poetry muses, there aren't enough ways to thank you: Lise Goett, your eye and heart were my midwives; Joseph Powell, I am ever grateful for the conversation and unflagging generosity; many thanks to Peter Zervos for sharing a love of meter; and to Hariclea Zengos for the sisterhood; thank you DL for introducing me to the Captain of the Guard the summer of 2014. Natalie Bakopoulos, Carolyn Forché, Alicia (A.E.) Stallings, Margot McPherson-Balanos, Amalia Melis, David Mason, Katerina Iliopoulou, Debra Marquart, Rachel Hadas, Christopher Bakken, Alexandra Nikiforidou, Alexandra Halkias, Theodoros Chiotis, Jane Satterfield, you make the journey πολύτιμο. CK, DV, DiSalvo, geography is incidental; and to Korina, πάντα αγάπη. Thank you Kate and Mark, and all the wonderful people at Red Hen Press, for another launch.

A very warm thanks to Cynthia Hogue, Rhina P. Espaillat, and Scott Cairns for their poems, example, and good words on this collection.

THURSDAY, 16

I awoke having gone through the history of the Death of History or rather the history of the History of Death (and this is no play on words).

—Odysseus Elytis, *Journal of an Unseen April*

for Nat

CONTENTS

III

A HISTORY OF TOO MUCH

I

One of those stones is precious.
It can change everything.
It can make the darkness shine.
It's the light switch for the whole country.

—Tomas Tranströmer, "Further In"

THE STARTLED DREAMS OF THE FALLEN IN SPRING

The spinach leaves are startling, the sun, too—
finally strong after the grey days and weighted blues.
The sun and the spinach greens startling
like the waft of scents coming down from the mountains.
Carpets of lavender from the Easter trees, *Paskalies*
and their aroma cover our broken pavements,
our streets where the homeless sleep.
But the brown hours of winter, the chill still
in our dreams wake us—I am not sure if this is
the pollen of sleep or the difficult breathing of spring.
After so much grief, the darkness has seeped into our dreams.
I see a gold-flecked bird, a ladder against a wall of vine-greens.
And on waking I remember the strange Lucite,
the climb to the child that startled me as I carried her down
to the ground, scents of the darkness and moist trees
kept me from falling with the girl in my arms.
I came down one Lucite rung at a time, fearing
like the thousands of fallen that I'd slip—I could see them
against the walls, on the dirt curled like caterpillars,
their dark-stemmed shapes over pavements, worm-like
in the midst of new greens. In my dream
there were other shapes, too. A woman
handing out clothes pegs ungenerously was startled
when I asked for more—she could only give me two that were green—
as the air surged with lemon blossoms,
and a gold-flecked bird perched above the unsaved,
their hands and arms stretched out from blankets, jutting twigs
flooding me with grief when V, a colleague,

walked on ahead, determined to outwalk the fetid scents.
I kept telling V she was walking too quickly, but this was a dream
and I couldn't stop her, or the man holding a child in his lap
startling me with his soft-worded *please,*
the curly-haired daughter he was holding, asleep.
Another colleague quit trying to keep me from falling.
In a great wind I kept leaning forward
he was relaxed and knowing while I,
unsure in the darkness, remembered B's lavender sprigs
still pungent in my pockets though I was now falling,
the gold-flecked pollen a dust on my lips
as my neighbor asked me, *Would you like some lemons?*
Yes I needed some lemons, this man had recently died but
he urged me to take them, their yellows lucent, startling,
more startling than anything I had dreamed.

THOSE DAYS

We woke almost excited
though not with joy, wakeful like an animal alert
to a danger it cannot see, but can sense

in the tension of the air those days we walked
straighter than usual, aware of the
smallest movements, the drug addicts leaning

into each other as if their spines had collapsed,
someone scratching at a scab. Unlike them
we kept walking,

ignoring our hurt, the garbage stench
like a rotting cat, trash piled up from the strikes
those days the refugees from Africa

could not spread their wares
as the pavements gathered the party youth
who hung their banners from statues and trees.

Even the statues wore stoic looks
as they bore their spray-painted mustaches and added nipples,
weary citizens like the rest of us

shouldering a weight while the outdated
revolutionary songs blared from megaphones
set up by the party youth who still cared

for Communist hopes and the lyrics
of Ritsos, the songs and ballads
of Theodorakis, today we think of those days

as long gone as we hand over change
to respectfully dressed men who apologize
for their begging and explain

they are desperate, with families. Today
it will take a small miracle to save us, we know
it's not enough to do our duty, pay our bills . . .

Those days . . . we will say if we are lucky
to grandchildren and young friends, *People died in Greece
not because of war, but because*

some didn't see the enemy, or recognize them in time.

THE EVENING THE REFERENDUM WAS REPEALED

The metro gates are down?
There was no announcement of a strike.
Someone lights a cigarette.
The usual, someone else shrugs, and starts to walk.
At least this gives us a chance to talk.
The parliament windows are lit
as if it were Christmas, but it's because
the country's fate is in the balance,
because armed guards
cross the street with shields.
The city's been shutting down for two years.
Even the protestors are fed up,
one with his face smeared white
to keep the tear gas from stinging
sighs, *This revolution's getting tiring.*
Someone else laughs,
the revolution has become a kind of joke.
Graffiti-smothered walls tell us,
FUCK THE EURO. FUCK THE IMF.
For some reason these two scrawls
have not been washed off.
Revolution is a sacred word
in Greece, it means there were always ways to resist,
the Greeks were good at this—
they resisted Mussolini,
they delayed the Nazi expansion.
In the end the war continued for everyone.

HEMORRHAGING MAP

Europe will shrink and disappear she said,
the banks and bankers have taken over,
and Europe's people, its heart, bled.
Europe will shrink and disappear, she said,
again, *its wounds are many and won't mend.*
Misled, its bodies bled until they were no longer
Europe; *it will shrink and disappear,* she said.
The banks and bankers have taken over.

SLOWLY

While things were happening very fast, and people were talking
all the time, sometimes yelling when there were protests—
people shouting to move out of the way when a Molotov was tossed,
a smashed windowpane splintered—we tried to slow down our thoughts,
we tried to think through each piece of the news as if
we were chewing on food that was difficult to swallow.
It was strange, too, how carefully we walked over the broken glass
as if these shards were precious, as if scattering them could hurt
the already scarred asphalt. It was strange because there was so much
glass to walk over that some days you forgot it was glass—
you imagined yourself in a gale storm ripping through
a country so that nothing was left unhurt. The storm ate through
sturdy buildings, even the stones of pavements, you could see
the iron insides of what kept things in place. We felt suddenly very small,
the way someone feels in a gale storm, and the larger and more bold
the headlines, the smaller we felt—even the pitch of television
voices shrunk us, things like getting out change for the metro or looking
at fallen leaves on the curbside took a long time—we kept looking
at those browns, strange, crushed greens, the veined skins, and forgot
we were standing in that small space of ours.

THE TAXI DRIVER LAMENTS

What's happening, did you hear?
I want to get home to catch the news tonight
but can't say no to someone who needs a ride
—there's no metro again?
There's always something.
We're losing our minds in all this.
But you know I'm a Socialist, I've never
voted for anything right-wing, ever, but
what's happened to him—he's a good guy
you know. I've had him in this cab
when he was the minister of education,
he's a good guy, I mean I like him
but something's wrong, how did he get us
into this crazy situation? I want to tell him,
I want to say we love you, the people
are with you—do you know what kinds
of real work I did with this cab
to get people behind his father? I was driving
all over the place, to my village every weekend,
rounding people up—you believe me
don't you? I mean no one wants a Fascist,
that's what this right-wing guy is, we'll be
doomed if he comes into power, he'll sell everything
but tell me, do you think he's being told
to do all this by someone we don't know about,
I mean, really, *who* is advising him?
You know I see over one hundred people a day
in this cab, I can tell you that right-winger
isn't going to make it,

the young people are all voting for small parties,
so he's not getting their vote either—
it's such a shame though, a tragedy—
why did it have to be like this? Is he ill?
He has us so confused. We're all going to end up in jail.
I mean how does he expect people to eat?
He keeps cutting everything—do you think
he really loves this country? I mean *does*
he feel what the people are feeling?
He has to know what people have done for that party,
people like me, we got his party into power
in the '80s, I came from Germany, now
my children are all in Germany and I've told them
not to come back, we've lost the game,
it's too late now. But why did this happen—
why did they do this? Even now,
even now people would help him,
he doesn't listen though—do you have any idea who
he listens to? Probably to his mother, okay
she's his mother, and he's alone now,
he can't trust anyone around him,
especially those ministers,
but he doesn't ask for help from the right people—
he *owes it to us* to tell us the truth.
I mean is he a traitor, do you think
he loves something else that he's not telling us about?
God needs to give us a hand here—it's too late for us
to do anything now, this is a beautiful country,
we love our country—you don't know

what I hear every day in this cab, people from all over—
we end up hugging each other,
I'm proud to be Greek,
I've always been proud of my country
and now I'm humiliated, we've all been.
He should have said from the beginning
that we didn't have any money, why did he lie to us?
—It makes you wonder, look at us now,
he's made us ashamed, *what did we do to you,*
I want to ask him, I just want to ask him that.

THE HISTORY OF TOO MUCH

There is too much here, the sapphire, the thistle,
the oregano blooms in June, everything extravagant—
the rich peat of what decays, the ruins that don't decay,
these especially are too much, the temples and statues
in their stark marble glow, that simplicity which is not simple at all.
This sheen of time, the wear of wars, the famine years
of Occupation, lucent as the columns standing stoic, Doric—
their weight has whittled the people: the weight of that antiquity,
of those stones, the grandeur and pride—too much
in this moment, this present crushed by the violence
of living with beheaded gods, and maimed still
beautiful torsos, the muscled limbs in chipped robes.
They plague our dreams, what was once achieved is now
incomplete, these pieces of the Golden Age aging
in the midst of traffic, too much, the yelling and honking,
the protests in the middle of everything—people are impatient—
how can anyone be patient, overwhelmed as they are.
Even the oregano's thick perfume, the sapphire sea,
remind people of extravagant loves and sacrifice, while here,
now, ghosts live on as gods and their impossibility.

MY ATHENS STREETS HAVE THIS TO SAY

Oh God, that's DARK, he says, but you're not afraid of God
just the carcass of hope and here on *Klathmonos*
watch a Gypsy selling staplers,
Kleenex packets and pop-up screwdrivers,
the pretty gypsy girls with their practiced smiles.
The man with red-dyed hair plays old rock songs
on an amplified guitar strapped around his skinny hips
singing as if they were new hits. Meanwhile
above all this is the lit Acropolis
in the midst of the clatter. Whatever hell
the news decides to televise, it stands a wonder
as police gather on corners, young guys
in uniforms a US college student called hot;
you nodded but what you're not saying is how much
she or any like her who come visiting
with their dreams from faraway places
make you want to say, *Like a difficult lover*
Athens is wanton but tender—her streets
perfume in spring, orange blossoms caress the pavements
and the toothless woman outside the cell phone store
knows it's sure to rain—give her an umbrella or talk to her
as if you were her lost most beloved, and know
she'll turn from you, bored by your surprise—
the scrawl of desperate slogans mark her.
She's used to passionate disappointments,
too used to them to care if you'll love or forget her.

THIS CITY

After C. P. Cavafy (& AES)

The ruins urge you to *find a new city*,
look for another shore. Even the broken finger
of a still white statue in the park points
westward. You could take that advice,
travel, find your way far from the hungry,
the shut-down stores, hope for another life.
But you are mesmerized by the ignited people
and that priest or bishop in the park,
missing half his finger (who knows what his story is,
a thrown rock aimed for the statue's face
hit his raised hand instead?)—they won't leave you—
the gouged marble, the graffiti scrawls,
the statue standing like something outraged
remind you, you who yearned to live beyond this,
that hope marked you, too.

FATHERLAND

My father's cracked vertebrae mean he walks in terrible pain this June.
Patrida, a Greek poet says, a word that would explode on the page this June.

I eat the greens my father liked to clean with lemons bought from the *laiki*.
This summer his spectacular Aegean is far away, the oregano, too, purple this June.

You've never had money so you don't know its taste, the villager says.
Children play ball and someone laments the record increase in suicides this June.

The broken Greek state announces we won't be getting our regular pay,
and protesting *Indignants* weep the stinging sprayed toxins in *Syntagma* this June.

Thyme wafts down the Attic hillside with acid rains. Listen to the pain,
a constant whisper on the subway trains. My father wants a Cretan wine this June.

Αδριαννα, a friend asks, *how will anyone get out of this crisis?*
I begin with *patrida* . . . a word, a country, the poem I am trying to write this June.

UNGODLY

You want to flee, but flee where? The urban concrete elsewhere
does not seethe, does not breathe the scent of carob trees.
Flee, you hear it everywhere, the taxi driver, the farmer at the *laiki*
tell you, *Go!* and are puzzled that you are still here,
you who could actually leave with your American passport.
Pack your clothes, leave behind the ruined lives, translate *home* into
longing, elsewhere you might lift your chin, live unburdened.

The government, the Americans . . . no one cares, the taxi driver complains,
and the farmer at the *laiki* selling you the sweetest pears, advises
to keep them fresh, *Eat them cold, nearly frozen.*
He shakes his head, murmurs *Ellada . . .* , this ancient land of rock cliffs,
seas that bleed their myths, Greece with its tales of flight
and light, returns and rebirths, keeps teaching the stubborn human lesson
still: the gods won't save you, neither will you stop wishing it of them.
After all, you are human and they are not.

PROMISE

11/2/2015 Syntagma Sq., Athens

I saw Gina at the gathering tonight—
she had been the first to encourage me
and took my hand when I defended my doctorate.
She's brilliant, a Poe scholar, and loves to talk about Cavafy.
Her son and husband both committed suicide
at different times in their lives, and I think Gina
never again went to that place in her heart that could hurt
in a way that would break it—she always talked in the first person
about places she visited and things she did—
When I was in Copenhagen, when I lectured at Columbia
she would say, when we knew those were the times
she had a family, in Copenhagen, and when she taught at Columbia.
Those tragedies left her by a window forever looking
to find the sky, and once she found a butterfly on the sill
motionless as she wrote; she thought it might be dead
until it lifted itself into the air, gold-patterned and black.
What she carried with her, what she taught us
was all in the literature she loved, in the fierce ways
she spoke of love, and death, and sex.

So when I saw her in the square at the gathering,
her eyes shining in a distant gleam, she nearly passed me
since it had been years, and she was being helped along
by a young woman who heard me calling her name.
People had gathered there to support the new government
elected after the hard austerity years.
The lights of the square were all on, and we could hardly move.
Some people had brought their children,
and I worried that they would get pushed and maybe hurt

because there wasn't enough room after a while.
People were strangely quiet, which isn't the usual way
the gatherings take place in *Syntagma*. Just months ago
the right-wing government passed a law
that would not allow large numbers to gather in places like the square.
Some people had written on placards that Greece
was in solidarity with Europe, that we were here
together, huddled, in our coats. It was cold
but our bodies were pressed against one another.
I was also thinking of the love I am involved with—I almost said
"*was* involved with," how convenient it would be
to use the past tense—let go of what could not be managed,
the promises we made, the risks we said we would take,
it's a heady thing when doubt makes those expectations seem foolish
though in this crush of people (so many people are gathered
here tonight), you want to give life a chance
like Gina who always speaks in the present tense.

ERASURES

Though we say love is the power
that bridges distances

countries have disappeared.

Alexander the Great
got lucky—

Mavros Kleitos, a devotee
accused him of letting the best die
to defend him
in a city now erased.

Kleitos was quickly killed
and the city ravaged,
left unnamed.

Alexander
on a drunken whim
almost lost everything.

Any doubt that greatness
cows enemies
(an idea loveless but alive
even to him
who encouraged
marriages of difference)
would have done him in,
would have let love in.

READING WITH ETHEL

Words opened their wands
—how I wanted to ask, can you imagine
such entrance, the nature of this red
loosened in mayhem?

Words opened and the skinned page
became praise—flesh does not
allow such freedoms, you could, though,
meld the grammar, resist.

II

But how can we hope to save ourselves in that which is most fragile?

—Italo Calvino, "Lightness"

SKIN

My father is almost tender as his skin turns the color of browned leaves. Sometimes he catches himself excited to hear from me, though he is someone who has never known how to express feelings, especially happy ones, since the last world war—in the last century when his skin was young as new leaves—singed what was tender in him. After an exploded bomb charred his arms, he never stopped hurting. He kept people at a distance. Anyone could be the enemy, even his wife who wouldn't leave him, though he made a habit of making her feel crushed. But *of his flesh,* as the saying goes, I left, and hardly thought of him though I would notice my skin—the spotted browns of crusting leaves that marked my flesh like his. I would sometimes call, and we'd talk over the safe distance of the Atlantic, and he would occasionally catch himself off guard and say something more than skin deep. Strangely, it was skin that brought us to the subject—I was saying I had burned my palm on the gas stove, watched my flesh blister and remembered his story of honey, how it saved them in the mountains during war, how it kept them alive, that and garlic and slogs of wine. Remembered when a bullet had lodged in a soldier's flesh he said they basted, the wound covered in honey and honey-soaked rags. This (he actually laughed) was their medicine! Garlic was also good. One soldier got through an amputation with cloves of it swallowed with wine. They got him drunk, had him biting a bullet when they cut the gangrened leg at the knee. Honey stopped the bleeding. *Honey stopped the blistering,* I say over the phone when I let my father know I remembered his story. *I spread the whole jar of it over my hand.* It was almost miraculous, the sticky and abundant feeling cutting through pain.

BECAUSE THE NEWS WAS BAD

I picked up honey from a man who didn't give receipts,
dark curls of homemade pasta with *xaroupi*.

The kitchen isn't warm but there's tea for evenings
when I sit in it, and wine that's not expensive.

These accomplishments are so small I don't know
if I can even use the word for what they celebrate

though it is an occasion when you find the woman still there
who sells honey and fruit at the stand on *Panepistimiou*.

She was there for years, bagging the healthy-looking
apples and oranges and bananas and the cherries and plums

when they were in season, her rough hands
with their polished nails, dark reds or pinks were the colors

I remember, I think it was important for her to polish her nails.
The honey she sold was the best and cheapest buy,

it came from Tripoli she said, the man who had the bees
delivered only certain times a month. Behind the fruit stand

the heroin addicts shoot up on the sidewalk,
you sometimes recognize the faces, they're the same ones

waiting for the pushers who don't always look much different
from the users, maybe quicker on their feet, more alert.

The police are rarely around. I go to work every day
feeling as if that is already something to manage, the trip to work

not an accomplishment in the way receiving an award might be.
Kiki wrote me that she is reading Rimbaud, "delighted"

by the poems. I don't think it is a verb frequently used
to describe Rimbaud, but it says a lot about perspective.

Kiki also said that the horizon felt empty
and the line between being devastated and saved

was thinner than anyone realized so we really can't talk about
a celebration or an accomplishment though we enjoy

the wine and honey and poetry.

FIRST AUDITION

In the hazed windows—tomorrow's market wares,
plastic containers and cotton underwear stacked on one store shelf.
No takers this time of night, and I'm thinking she's unaware,
on stage in another hemisphere, reciting lines, herself
the daughter Iphigenia. And like Agamemnon listening to her plea,
the sages will decide, judge the worth of her words, and grief.
She's giving of her heart, fighting Calchas' decree
while I, the mother, walk the streets without relief.
Despite the hour, the drunks, the one man chewing on a rusk
with something close to lust, I can't stop thinking of her part—
what grim fate brought this man to his single crust?
I pass parked vans, tomorrow's meat in a lit shop, dark
chopping blocks clean behind the glass, see the skinned lamb last,
imagine butchers making cuts, how the blood will run, how fast.

CLOTHING THE DEAD

My friend who lost her beloved stared at the bottom of the steps where he lay in the early morning, his skull cracked. Later there were more people. The undertaker wanted some clothes. The undertaker, a large man too quick to wear his sunglasses before leaving, was not pleasant. *A tie, jacket, socks, shoes*, he said. Someone closer to my friend shook her head and said instead, *Something cotton and light, and nothing synthetic, no jacket. Oh*, my friend breathed, *I can't believe it*, when she had to go back up the steps he had fallen down. I washed out cups, a woman spoke of time, a tiny spoon fell and I picked it up.

STOPOVER IN BADEN-BADEN

My face sweats
in the warm current
batting through
the open window.
Everything is closed
when I arrive.
Everything is
in a foreign tongue.
An impatient teller
and a weary man, someone
who has no idea how
he is going to get a sleeper,
are talking.
The German teller repeats
in accented English,
I just gave you information.
The African-American pleads,
*I can't stand for hours
after a flight from the States.*
The teller is not sympathetic.
The weary traveler says,
*It's just stupid
that I can't book a sleeper.
Just so stupid!*
In the darkness
those faces reappear—
the tired African-American,
the irritated German.
It was a short trip

and the train half-empty.
I didn't have a ticket
because it was late
though the teller
seemed to think I could explain this
if anyone asked
in the pungent
full-moon night
on a train nearly empty
with torn seats
where a grass scent
wafts through the window,
Germany's last war
in the last century lingering
in the fields and breeze.

EXILIC

After Daniel Simko

Collapsed
endings
in a field of snow

passengers
clutch bags

in a faraway land
the scent is damp.

INVITATION

Tell me what you want, he said,
it was a lovely line, the call of a Siren.
I packed thin stockings, a dress,
pretty underwear.
It didn't matter that like Odysseus
I would find unexpected weather,
that it was suddenly cold and the clothes with me
were with me because we had met
in warmer weather.

I paid attention, stayed alert,
—it kept Odysseus alive
being careful of his whereabouts.
I thank my hosts,
their generosity is never expected.
I'm used to being a guest,
treated as if my tastes might differ.
But when I say what I want (finally at ease)
my preferences are mistaken
for something not offered.

My stockings and underwear were useful.
So were the gloves and hat I brought,
but he is unfamiliar. *Tell me what you want*
is still a beautiful line; he used it perfectly,
my clothes were irrelevant.

REFUSING TO BE DEMETER

No, I don't like that myth, the way it brings the bled flesh
and death so close; I don't want or need the lesson—
I know it well and prefer to leave behind the grief,
let Persephone have her time with Hades or Hal, eat or not eat
the pomegranate. I did what I could, scoured every inch of what I loved
through her gaze—all of it, the blooming ground, acrid and sweet,
the burgeoning growth, while like winter I gradually stiffened,
weather whittling what I once knew to be me, and in this chill
the calamity—limbs torn in the sheer element of lament.

No, I refuse this story, I who am not a god,
I who cannot follow her anyway, bound to nature's law.
Why not sit to what I can enjoy—I could eat the fruit myself.
October coats the air, the temperature has dropped, the offerings are ripe.

WINTER, WHY?

He is morose doing homework—
the boy those years ago who looked up
to question December's clouds.
Or maybe after months of cold
this child couldn't help but wonder at
the still grey days
and then—I don't remember, I might have said
the seasons bring betrayals with their gifts,
for more than rain, or grey, when all is rain
and grey and homework days we hate the most,
they mean to teach us of the fickle ways
the temperature will change—
what you learn and still don't know
sweet boy, these too you'll miss,
so love that stubborn math stubbornly.
It's teaching you how keen the chill will be,
and also, as your mother said,
on that road of the dead
we happened to be driving on
that led to the cemetery,
there's a florist who takes his time
doing a job like the rest of us,
though he's a florist on *Anapafseos*,
a road named *Rest* that goes in two directions.

BECAUSE HAPPINESS IS TEMPORARY, UNCERTAIN & HOSPITABLE

Rain made up the night and our goodbyes and the extreme kindness of how people told each other of the time we shared together. R said to wake him before 4 a.m., he would put on his shoes and take down my heavy bag. It was terribly heavy and I couldn't get it down the stairs on my own. After sharing the work we had all done in the weeks together we were tired and satisfied and people read of their pain and betrayals, saying we were there in the workshop to speak and shape these feelings.

Before I dozed off the rain continued in a steady pouring—the open windows let in the humidity and the light from an opposite apartment where earlier I watched a thin woman who gathered dried laundry and a young child who entertained himself as she folded the towels and socks. There was no message from him. I looked for one before I slept. How little it would have cost to let me know he was thinking of me (if he was thinking of me)—but then I didn't want to use the verb, or maybe I did—what anything might cost seemed to have been part of what we'd learned in these weeks. I would certainly have been helpless if R had not put on his shoes and half-awake dragged my bag at 4 a.m. down the very narrow stairs.

The cobbles of the Freiburg alleyway shone like gem surfaces, three brass squares of death lodged between the stones in front of the building where I waited. The rain glistened in the headlights of the approaching cab. I could see the names, JULIUS VEIT, KATHARINA VEIT, ANTONE VEIT, a family. Deported, *deportiert* it says, in 1940. Julius, *tot* 28.12.1940, must have died soon after. Antone, murdered, *ermordet* 1942 in Auschwitz. I got into the cab before I could read what happened to Katharina. The driver motioned that we were blocking the alleyway. He took me to the bus station where, already exhausted, I listened to two young women speaking in Spanish. The word *dinero* was repeated, and their laughter. The costs of our traveling, the trips that are far from what we know best or know at all, depend so much on small kindnesses. *Don't sweat the small stuff*, M said—this vernacular surprising from M who is Romanian. She had visited a sperm bank in Poland and had just had a child. She had called the cab for me because I don't speak German. The cab driver didn't speak English, he pointed to a lighted digital meter to show me the fare. He too helped me lift my bag. I lined up with other passengers. At the airport we were told to declare anything liquid, sharp, or dangerous. I could have declared my heart, liquid, sharp and dangerous—dangerous as the misstep that would have sent R tumbling down the stairs.

My stay had been full of instances when I was forced to do better than what seemed possible. It was not measurable, like the cost of the cab or the shirts with gaudy plastic baubles I bought for M's children. M's daughter spoke to her in whispers. She wanted the shirt with the baubles. M held her very fair three-month-old brother. The beautiful baby had Danish genes. M had been given the bios of two sperm donors, a carpenter and a teacher. She said she'd asked for the teacher but couldn't be sure whose sperm she got. M lives in poverty, though she gets money from the German state. I tried to avoid conversations about her finances. She was livid with criticism for what she believed was a preferential system. I didn't always agree. I did say the costs of having any child, let alone two, in a southern European country would be a lot higher. M insisted, *People are friendlier and more humane in the south*. Again I didn't always agree. We went for a swim in the lake my last day, and I took pictures of her daughter who went into the water with me. She said she didn't have any photographs of her children and wanted to remember them young, also that she was so much better since she gave birth to her son. *The walls breathe*, she said and meant it.

I keep seeing the pure glee in her daughter's face, M's perfectly contented smile, and remember a German acquaintance who told me he didn't go to a concert of a famous Greek singer on tour because it would have made him weep to hear her sing.

MISSING THE PLANE

I watch a man being told the Toronto flight has already left.
He keeps repeating, *1:00 p.m.?*
He isn't angry, just bewildered, says someone at work
was supposed to have helped him with this—
It's going to be an 18-hour trip for me with two stops,
my left leg already feels cramped and I'm tired, I try not to
imagine the hours. I'll read poetry and try to sleep.
I was traveling for love, the best reason for any journey.
The man who missed his flight is a kind of premonition.
The ground steward promised to help him out, but
his perspective has changed, his sense of time and expectations,
even his idea of how to ask for directions.

IN A POMEGRANATE TIME

We found each other unexpectedly, unplanned, we kissed extravagantly.
I had not known this language, the continents it crossed extravagantly.

Tell me of your old loves, Phoebe who wooed you, Niki who wanted you
to speak of how you made love, and that you left them so extravagantly.

It is again the pomegranate season, the ripened fruit skins open red seams
like mouths, gorgeous with plump seeds, ready to be eaten extravagantly.

You liked our rifts in conversation, not the gap in time zones—or me
asleep and you about to sleep but awake and looking for me extravagantly.

The charged hemispheres left us with hour differences, and rioting synapses.
Talk was an aphrodisiac, like the funny smile you withheld extravagantly.

I didn't want the complications, but your world had a largesse I thought
rare like democracy and romance, a betrayal that developed extravagantly.

Let me describe the ravage, the ways a bitten thing might live its grief,
a Demeter in sudden winter, or me in a country falling apart extravagantly.

And you? Will you go back to the coves and short notes, the fruit seasons?
Ask another Phoebe or Niki how deeply they loved and lost extravagantly?

Let yourself be whispered to, and conjure goddesses, call out my name as it
grows foreign, the fig or *Figette* lost in the Aegean we swam extravagantly.

DEAR

Dear H,
the peppers were lovely,
their skins remind me
of your thighs.

I'm up in the middle of the night.
It is your eyes
I like.

I am unquenched
dear H, imagining you
licking saltwater
from the breasts of goddesses.

Dear H,
it isn't the quiet that scares me,
it isn't even my creaturely heat—
it's my cravings.

The peppers
on their fine vines
were perfect
and I ate them.

XXX . . .

Every day there was a line, sometimes two,
they ended with a group of kisses,
Xs that I counted on, and counted
every day there was a line, sometimes two.
Those Xs grew the more expected
the nights of hours, and days of days Xed
every day there was a line, sometimes two.
They ended with a group of kisses.

THE RETURN

You dreamed of stuffing the minimum
into a bag, quickly, like any refugee
without much sense of where
the traveling would lead you.
Some books, maybe your creams,
the soft boots, and your jeans.
So already you are better off
than any refugee, you can choose.
You have creams,
you have soft boots,
but you are tired of the overly optimistic voices
in this new world,
the cheerful recordings
and impossibility of getting a person
to speak with. Remember,
when you return
the voices, even the scents,
will bring disappointment.
Faces heavy with history
will make you feel you are back
in a homeland you know well, without hope,
without the certainty of those unfamiliar voices
who speak with such familiarity,
and you will be desperate.

KINDS OF PLACES

A friend tells you of her children's colds.
I say something about
my daughter's being unclear
of where she wants to live
though we are asking other things
—I mention a sign in Yakima,
BLUE GROUSE RESTAURANT,
how polite everyone was on the trip.
The weather kept changing,
apples hung ripe on their trees
and mushrooms grew everywhere.
You had to be careful
to recognize which were poisonous.
Some, like the chanterelles
grew in the mountains,
oyster mushrooms appeared
out of tree bark,
distressed and decaying wood—
the kinds of places you might overlook.

THE WOUND, A MOUTH, AN EYE

The heart is the toughest part of the body.
    —Carolyn Forché

The wound is an eye,
    also a mouth, always an opening.
There are many
    openings in
the ways to phrase a devastation.
    Excuse me
    for intruding begins
    a sentence already kneeling,
    and still polite.
I am embarrassed,
    says another *with all due respect,*
    for asking you to give
    anything you can.
While most give nothing
    a woman scrounges
    through her bag
    opening it wide,
    her silver bangles jingle
    and two large rings sit
    on the hand searching.
    She smiles at the person
    waiting, *I'll give you . . .*
    she starts, *I'll give you whatever*
    I find here.
    Her spare change softens
    the litany of pleas,
    though everything

is a wounding the openings
don't close.

THIS SURFACE

—I was looking closely at the woman's skin
on the metro

wanting my lover's touch,
there was a moon that night and a question of
whether or not I had bought a ticket.

They were checking and I managed
to get by—
I often wondered if this wasn't

a matter of sheer will, the getting by.
A voice was asking,
Do you have 50 cents to spare?
Do you have something?

And a good-looking man, and a grandmother
seemed threatened.
Just some cents . . . I heard again.

I'd spent 15 euros on a sweater
and had been drinking
with friends, so what was 50 cents?

But I kept walking,
the anonymity
of a woman's stepping outside the metro
in clear pantyhose and a matching bag

was what I wanted,
that indifference of the moon,
of having nothing to lose—

that what I cared for was enough.

LET YOURSELF FORGIVE

Why turn from the promise, the pleasure,
that kiss you wanted to relive—
it left you a taste, a hunger with no measure.
Why turn from the promise, the pleasure,
an expectation you hoped to treasure.
Don't be upset, please—let yourself forgive
your turn from the promise, the pleasure,
that kiss you wanted to relive.

THE ROAD

I could have driven through a red light,
gone skidding, the car thrown
and me strangely okay with whatever
might happen because it didn't feel
especially dangerous
even if in my night driving I was exhausted
and tense about the distance it took
to show him the spectacle,
a tragedy in an ancient theater.

The costumes were all off, the actors
overplayed their parts, and afterwards
we kept looking for a place to eat.
There was only a ramshackle kind of café.
The young girl serving us
had to cross the road to bring the food.
Cars whipped past, you had to be aware
of how fast they were going, and it was night
and I was in love with that road.

III

World,

throw it off then! Throw it!

It doesn't matter what covers you when the sky sleeps.

In the light you are a dangerous place.

—Monica Sok, "Nocturne"

YELLOW WIND

Like a fairytale powder it covered the pavements, leaves, balconies, the shoes I left out, it was in the cat's fur, brooms, coating windshields, hardened candle wax, towels I forgot to take in and shake out. I watched the dust float, the film settling over railings and windowpanes, looked above to where pines moved in a wash of pollen and sand from the Sahara blowing in, and with it were people from the Middle East with its taste on their tongues, the people of one thousand and one nights in tents or without tents, their clothes full of desert grains, a reddish powder under their nails and in their hair, a sand from the empire of Sasanian kings. They can't shake it out despite their waterlogged arrivals. They can't untaste the dust or wash their hands and skin of it or lighten tongues and mouths too full of what has drowned. This wind is thick and sticks, a red like rust is in the yellow this spring, the spring at the end of fairytales when wands and good fairies sprinkle a soft gold that coats Snow White or Cinderella or Hansel and Gretel; made happy for the tale, for the fairies, we forget Scheherazade began each Arabian Night to save her life.

1.

Stranger-man, stranger-man . . . Are you looking in my mirror, man?

It is the word I won't use (what are the words I won't use, the names I could name?)—
Words have their fashions like the ism in Fascism, a notorious fetishism I will outgrow. My cave of self caved into itself where my father still stands in the mirror, reflecting me looking to be as he yanked the brush from my hand. I'm leaning toward him in impulse and nerve those adolescent years ago, slapped.

We want the other—*an*other (not *any* other)—to touch so we can be two. Touched, we can get beyond our single currencies, and mirrored selves. The man on the metro with a fallen jaw is carefully belting his pants and trying to speak. He is struggling and people look away. The stranger-man is trying very hard to be heard, and maybe has not been touched in a long time.

The stranger-man keeps looking to see who might answer his plea, but people are unsympathetic, like Ms. Clayton in a small schoolroom in Bangkok. Ms. Clayton smacked my knuckles with a wood ruler when I recited multiplication tables and skipped the 7s. *Stand straight* she commanded, as the ruler came down on my raised hand. I can stare at the mirror far too long, trying to see this punishment part.

He is so sweet, this stranger-man with his permanently fallen jaw. I want to hold his hand. A migrant opposite me is darting looks his way, agitated that no one seems to be helping, as the stranger-man makes his determined efforts to say what he is trying so hard to say. *I can't hear you,* a guy on the metro says with earphones in his ears, though he has heard enough to say this. He stands opposite the sweet, challenged man who tries again to speak as his knees lean into each other, and he pulls up his belted pants. He keeps making his awkward way as the metro moves at its clipped pace. He makes his way to someone seated and repeats his question about a stop and where to get off. The seated man answers and promises to help out. A woman stands, concentrated on not looking. Like the man with the earphones in his ears, she has sized up the man with the fallen jaw and decided he is spoiled goods while the stranger-man says *thank you*, to whatever the guy with the earphones happens to say, even if it's his repeated *I can't hear you*, which really means, *I can't have you need me*, which he doesn't say.

2.

—Write dangerously there on the precipice, the pages are thin-skinned— be more dangerous (I was taught to keep damage private), to keep from dangerous drivers. I can't stop staring at the pretty woman's exposed arms, their pearl-sheened skin—the stranger-man with his fallen jaw, the legless woman selling Kleenex packets for a euro at the streetlights, are *trying* very hard to keep from the precipice—

the accident in the dark
is the dark—*didn't you see me coming?*
Each person thought
they had the right of way.
I'm afraid to revisit the site,

I'm afraid I'll revisit the site.

Things could be as simple as an exchange at a hairdresser's—

Will that be all for today?
Could I have your phone #?
Do you need my phone #?
I need to access you on the computer.

I don't want to be accessed.
Well, have a great day.

Things could be as simple as a body sweating, exploded in scents inside a crowded metro, not easily accessed. In a crowded Athens train people are staring into each other's faces. Some are bouquets, some labyrinths of these Athens days. I wonder if the stranger-man will manage. I wonder if the loud guys will trip him up on his precipice, as he makes his way to the escalators. Sometimes the sweat is thick. Sometimes I know the person in front of me has not washed in days.

Aside from the day, or inside it, a war thrives in the blistering flesh sweats. In the wet skin scents I consider my lost border, its humid languor. So many years ago a wide-eyed treasured child, slipped from between my opened thighs. I touched her forehead and thought her eyes could see air. Now my lover gazes up at me. My hands are in his curled hair. What body takes in the other without a heart-scream of lost contour, a civil war in the downpour, the sudden desert heat that is also a dry-sand pain—picture my language floods, its delicacies, an elaborate summer under a repulsive childhood moon.

3.

There is a melded rapture in the rupture—*Dear body, you are going to betray me at my moment of deepest need, at that moment when I am most in love and living. And you'll be cunning, too. It may not happen quickly, but it will feel that way. I am staring at a casket and the candlelight is thick. The flowers are white and the body has lived a full life.*

Drive light, said the symphony. *Here is a detour, a sharp pin turn.* Lust is blue and frantic.

Then there's what comes in the interim. What happens when the body makes inroads, takes its self apart as earth drinks, this will be its fate anyway, so invite it in. Stare at the crushed fruit skins, the green rot. Death is indifferent. Death takes the body, *any* body, and breathes its earth scent. I wish I could undo my undone shirt, unstitch the heat seam—my self or that sweet man's body he clothed so carefully is an overture coming apart, embarrassed and persistent.

Dear stranger-man with the fallen jaw, what are you struggling to say with such polite attention? The request you make across a dirty metro floor might as well be the space of any number of exploded countries, the musk scents, the waves of people (my father still stands in my way with unabashed disdain) hardly promise more than an accident of bodily collision. But you don't stop your hesitant pacing despite the stony faces, despite the one with the earphones who barely looks your way to say, *I can't hear you*, you still thank him. What worlds do you see in that blank face?

LUNAR

Potassium boils up from the earth's core. I'm on a road of accidents and the blackened silver heart. An abandoned hotel is full of rheumatic patients and the chamomile rampant. We listened to the tiny river song. Starving puppies licked my fingers of crumbled egg whites in the chamomile-filled air. Stamatina spoke of an astrology site—*the female will suffer and the man will feel burdened.* There's a blood moon, an ékleipsis of the failed and abandoned. We were retreating from the earth's shadow over a veiled moon's eye. When they breathed, the puppies' rib cages opened like accordion pleats. I gave them what I had, which wasn't enough.

COMING DOWN THE MOUNTAIN BEFORE DARK

The car had gas but maybe not enough,
a man who sat, a distance
from the pump, was nonchalant about my
question of the way—how long,
how far—he took his time
since time, it seemed,
was on his side, or on this mountain side
his life was fixed by seasons and their rhythms.
While I was always in some hurry,
a barely uttered fervor to beat the fear
that I would miss my chance
to reach my stop, and there find some respite,
from what I thought, as I came down
the curves of sheer rock heights
all bathed in blue-glazed light.
Black crows flew high above
the silvered trees, a clutch of women passed
a roadside icon stand where some soul lost a life
and someone kept a wick alive,
reminder of a he or she who'd slipped,
veered off or fallen from the cliff
I was so rapidly driving past—it left
a shiver down my back to think
how unexpectedly all falls to dark—
the trees lose their clear shapes, the sun slips
down the mountain ridge, and
in its spreads of reds a single clump of bush
or sudden trunk is etched against a burning sky
—I wanted to find my way

before the pitch of black
would hide these narrow, curving twists,
the way a village street appeared, and then
the open asphalt road again—some shops
waved by, a butcher's sign,
swathes of forest pine.
While I was anxious at the wheel
the breaths of air slid down my arms,
the hours ahead would bring me home,
I should relax, enjoy the ride,
but I was tense, my bearings lost.
I might forget the way, it was this heavy sense
that left me quite afraid—I slowed to ask
a group of men sitting at a roadside bend
if this was right, the turn I took.
The light was almost gone,
the road now dark.
A man chewing on a piece of gristle
kept nodding *yes* while I
wishing I could enjoy the meal with them,
instead, impatient, alone tonight,
since it was night,
strained hard to see the road ahead,
more flat but still unlit,
and named the scents that filled the dark,
lavender and thyme, the sudden stench
of *copria* that fertilized the fields.
I let them in, let night wash through,
but feared the lure. I'd hoped to keep ahead

—of what? The dark? Yet here it was.
There was a truck in front,
the passing often blinding lights
raced by, it wouldn't take much
to lose my grip as I kept gauging where I was,
sometimes too near the truck,
or swerving to the middle of the road.
I realized the threat, like sex
and felt a sudden thrill, remembered
a praying mantis, the bee it caught
inside a blossom's heart—it ate with such intent,
consumed the body till there was nothing left.

GATE E2

Port of Piraeus

There's the noise of municipal trucks,
a straggle of Salvation Army workers,
some photographers, the seagulls.
There are stories of the wait for the border
to open up, the wait (after having made it
on dinghies to Greece) also filled with cellophane-
wrapped sandwiches, bottled water, sometimes fruit.
But mostly there is just talk and the waiting,
seagulls and the sea and the children who play
or complain while their mothers gather around
a sheet we spread for them to draw
houses and trees. Yassin's shy yellow
keeps to the lines of a tractor.
Aasma next to him scoops up potpourri.
The colored flakes stick to her fingertips
as she gathers bits in an empty balloon.
We've brought balloons, markers and crayons
and Alicia's made a solution of dishwashing liquid.
The children loop circles out of pipe cleaners,
dip them into suds and blow bubbles,
the orbs stretching as they gauge their breaths.
Watching them float, some adults laugh
when the shapes linger.

OBLESSIVE ACHE

My sentence
never finds
closure
because
you taught me
oblessive
has *bless*
in the middle
splitting the "ive"
(my "I've ...")
from the "O"
(your "Oh ...")
of what could become
obsessive
or possessive—
a debt
to what is
more than
the miss
in my missive
is history I've wished
beyond me.

THE STRANGER JOY

After the teeming sadness
After the sun reflected warmth in a hotel blankness
After I stared at the back of his head of curls
After we kissed fleetingly
After he told me of the Angel of Death
After the air took on weight
After I dressed in silence
After breathing in the sheets' stale tobacco
After listening to the faint sound of passing cars
After the walls of windows splintered
After I knew I could walk the next block alone
After waiting to be offered water
After my brain split in a vast galaxy
After I lost myself in the impossible stars
After I asked for help
After realizing there was nothing in the room
After I tried to kneel
After he laughed himself to sleep
After joining him at the bar
After I found my way
After giving him the gifts
After I waited
kissed fleetingly
in the teeming sadness
with the Angel of Death
breathing in the sheets' stale tobacco
listening to the faint sounds of passing cars
realizing there was nothing in the room
my brain split in a vast galaxy

asked for help
waited to be offered water
tried to kneel
dressed in silence
stared at the back of his head of curls
joined him at the bar
the walls of windows opposite me splintered
the sun reflected warmth in a hotel blankness
the air took on weight
I waited
lost myself in the impossible stars
giving him the gifts
he laughed himself to sleep
I found my way
knew I could walk the next block alone
after that, only after that, could I say I was okay.

PLATEIA MAVILI

But will anyone who hears ever understand / That endless talking signals the end?
    —David Lazar

1.
You need to think about something else.
What will happen next? The country. Him.
You want him. You hope the country will save itself.
You think about both,
about what hasn't worked—
you mean the country
but you're talking to him
and he's talking of you not listening,
you are listening, but to what he's not saying.
This is also happening in the country—
a lot of people are talking, it's easier
when so many people are talking to think
about something else.

2.
You look at the temperature: 10°C,
a video on the metro's plasma screen.
The flat voice on the PA
names the next station, you sent a message
at each stop, a kiss
if only in your head. You did that
so he would know
no matter the station, street, or time of day
the pigeons you watched peck at thrown bread
on Plateia Mavili were intent, quick to move
and oblivious of traffic.

3.

If you sit long enough in the sun
on the corner of Plateia Mavili
on an early February morning you can
sit with nothing in your heart,
at least you'll tell yourself that.
Nothing, you say aloud, but no one hears you
because on Mavili
people are concentrated on getting themselves
wherever they are getting themselves
though one young woman at the corner
keeps doing a pirouette.

4.

He convinced you to give yourself
to the fountains' spray
wetting the tables and pavement
on Plateia Mavili. You listen to the smokers
at the kiosk, the woman
talking to the waiter,
the conversation scraps (about money
withdrawn, receipts,
today's Euro-group meeting)
—today when history is being made
or unmade, you are barely able to move
from your stool at the café
on Mavili. He convinced you,
the wet stains are all you look at.

THE HOUR OF THE DUMPSTERS

The cold is night wrapped,
the cat stretches and trees inhale—

Trucks pick up the trash,
mechanical and loud.

Your love's close friend has died,
a poet. You want to tell him it is the hour

of the dumpsters, that you wake up
in heat in the coldest month of the year

and like the news, the dumpsters
continue to churn the refuse

as the day starts to break.

WHAT I WISH MIGHT BE REAPED

In the pasture that is my house,
unkempt things—

an unmade bed,
things not picked up
like expectation,

a slip I forgot
in my lover's bed—
the nights and days I might have
tried to explain.

What did any of it mean?
A proximity
to what will be gone?

—He will tell me
so simply
of a need to make dinner,
get groceries

while I, in this pasture
want
a word, his attention—tell me how
to speak of this.

GAZE

Look at the change
the rain swept my way.
The air is a stain.

My nails remind me
of my grandmother's hands.
I still fit into my pants.

And when I slip this skirt
over my closed lids—the cut
and colors are what you stare at.

Look then.

Look at me washing
my favorite underwear
as the heat strips me.
The heat, the words, too,
left what's left.

THE GOODBYES

I want to tell you about saying goodbye to C,
a goodbye in an era of goodbyes.
In the red-inflected winds and days near sea
as the euro sank, we drank incessantly
and it was good, but C was fired
and did not know where she would go
in that summer of heat and drink
and terror too—everyone with an opinion
but no solution—it made us think
of what had brought us to this brink,
a disposition or indifference—*Cast a cold eye*
On Life, on Death, says Yeats, yet C
packed boxes with great care, labeled each,
knew what had gone to whom, the books
and clothes with me, a couch and bed
and stove with another friend.
The country had lost its way from where
we could or might still hope but we still went
to vote. C brewed sage tea,
I did a supermarket run in case
our Euro-world might cease to be.
Then C told me her watch was broken in a dream,
her sunglasses, too. She was lifting boxes,
ticked off a list of labels like POESIE as she described
the glue she used, that the lenses stayed
smeared with it, and she couldn't see.
The boxes, heavy and thickly taped, piled up
in my basement. We knew
when we would later speak of this

across the wide divide of time,
we'd somehow manage to speak of this.
For now C sautéed eggplant with tomatoes
for our evening meal, fried onion and basil leaves.
She had given me her best wines to keep,
Save them for a special day, she said.
One was a *Kir-Yianni* rosé, my favorite.
There were also two bottles of champagne
we drank the night before she left.
It was a lovely evening on the balcony
when we spoke of lost loves, and books—
how we loved our lost loves, how they disappeared
like countries, *I don't want to leave Greece*
but things can change, she said.
We spoke too of our goodbyes
to projects we didn't finish, the ways we felt
such lust for them, and then like lust
they faded even if we spoke of them for a very long time,
and of Proust, of teaching in the classroom,
how that too was coming to an end, and C
would be on her way to Cévennes.
I have no choice, she said again,
and added, *but it's okay*.
We talked some more of the Euro-group meeting
that evening after five months of meetings,
which was another kind of lust, and that night
I dreamt of a broken Barbie
someone had thrown into the back of my car.
I remembered how much I loved my dolls.

In a childhood of forgotten homes
how I lay my Ken on top of my Barbie
and had them kiss—there were stories I made up
of lives in pink Mattel houses in a faraway land,
and remembered all the dolls I kept
in different states of dress and undress, some
whose hair I cut, one with a missing hand,
a box of them I don't think I ever threw away.

SEA

We buried Mihali today, we buried him
at noon, in the heat of August
in the early afternoon
with his mother wailing over the casket,
her eyes bruised from so much crying.
It was a record-temperature afternoon
and people came in black,
some quiet despite their raw looks.
We could not believe we were burying Mihali
who strode so firmly through his life,
who walked into the nearby hills
to take in the span of the city,
his laugh raucous and wide,
a laugh that pulled you out
of your own life to feel something even larger
than him, and solid like his hands
that could clasp you fully
when he wrapped them around you
or held your face between the world of his palms.
You could let go with Mihali,
you could let yourself fall and know
he would gather you up.
For him to suddenly die
is as if the sea you expect to see
in its azure and cobalt depths
is suddenly not there,
as if after walking the long hours
in the heat to reach its waves,
expecting the weight of your body

to be lifted in its satin embrace, a waft
like the scent of jasmine in rain
—all that keeps you walking in your despair,
sure of that sheer blue—
after all the sun,
after your exhausted endurance,
you find you're mistaken—
the road you're on is much longer,
drier and more yellow
and there's no glimpse of the sea, only earth
everywhere, and Mihali gone.

THESE DAYS

I hear names that want to be songs, Unés, Hussein, Narges, Lace, Fatima, Aqdas, Seisma, an applause of arrivals. Seisma clutches a bald doll, twirls it in a wrap of cloth. Aqdas wants a *jupe* for her birthday that will float from her hips. The world has opened up. Epics are folded in minutes. There is new fruit in the belly, a just-next-door now gone. Laundry dries over railings in the schoolyard and someone is telling of the tamarind and rosemary in her dreams. The breeze is rancid. Heniah's mother puts a hibiscus flower behind her ear, ladybird barrettes in Heniah's hair. She peels potatoes in a tin basin, says *tashakor* for the lipstick and sneakers. The children are clapping with volunteers, singing *Old MacDonald Had A Farm E-I-E-I-O . . .*

POEM IN PIECES, A LOG

On June 26, 2015, Alexis Tsipras, Greece's prime minister and SYRIZA party leader, announced there would be a referendum to decide whether the country should accept the terms of a new EU bailout proposal that called for more austerity. From Monday, June 30, capital controls were imposed on Greek banks. People could withdraw up to 60 euros a day.

i

I was teaching persona poems
on an island where
circumstances bigger
than anything we might do
kept us doing whatever we might do

I was teaching persona poems
and asked how personas help expand
the self, save it
from disintegrating

Gulls glide effortlessly through horizon, their lack of vertigo in a dive
kept me staring

I taught Tarfia Faizullah's *Seam*, notice the word clusters, I said, the repetitions, the
khaki-clad bodies that grow sinister, the word *bayonet*, also the color *green*
and the word *jasmine*

Like personas, repetitions help us speak when speaking feels
impossible, in such situations I am also practical

I am speaking now to my lover, trying to

Speak of difficulties

And the voice of a friend warns
. . . The alternative is there is no food . . . people can't take their medicine now . . .
imagine next week . . .

The Eurozone wants to teach the Greeks a lesson. *It's game over. The markets are*
all up. The negotiation tactics didn't work . . . done . . . they thought their holding out
could affect the markets . . .

So Europe never wanted to help us
Europe wants Greece to be a lesson

I'm with you. So. Now what? Who is going to finance the country? Who is going to do
it if not Europe?

[I am on the island teaching how to build a poem, my lover is with me . . . he has
come from afar and the horizon feels burdened. A difficult vertigo is making it hard
to lift the words, so to speak]

It sucks. But who is going to give us money?

When events break us I tell the class, look for the pieces, cluster them. K, who is
writing a memoir about her mother's rape and murder, nods

They should have done the referendum a month ago. When they could still pay pensions.
I got my salary, and tell him that it was a money transfer
. . . Your 3000 euros in the bank aren't even there . . . the banks are using it . . .

[my daughter is happy transportation is free since the referendum was declared]

The referendum shouldn't have happened. There's still a day . . . maybe they'll agree to
something . . . all those old women trying to get their 100-euro pensions for the month
are the people his socialism was supposed to protect!

. . . the idiots on TV are talking like it's some minor inconvenience . . . the IKA health
director says, "Don't be that way . . . Things like this happen." The arrogance! . . .

I'm owed 20,000 . . . and who knows when I'll get it . . . and

[my daughter is going to a conference called Democracy Rising, well-known names
from Hellenic Studies programs in the States have come to speak. It is summer and
some of them are on vacation]

There was no worse timing . . . after 5 months of talks there isn't a cent in the banks . . .
we're going to say NO to the money they're going to give us? Otherwise what? Other-
wise we'll starve . . . what the fuck . . . I'm telling you I was with them . . . but it didn't
work out . . .

[they're going to squash him and us with him . . .]

To sign the deal we need a prime minister. In 2 weeks there will be nothing left in the
banks . . . nothing in the banks and a toppled prime minister . . .

ii

On the island I walk to the port town of Gavrio
and buy toilet paper, I heard it was toilet paper that ran out first in Argentina in

2001, someone in Athens says the shelves where the toilet paper is stacked were almost empty but it was cheese and olives, toothpaste and sunblock I came back with

One woman in line at the ATM snapped, *And he wants to be a Europeanist . . .*

iii

The winds are a blue sea shawl of filled current

Here the horizon is horizon

What bruise of cloud color

K showed me my empty bathing suit had blown to her side of the balcony, she took a picture of its pomegranate skin, and said, *That's not the color either,* pomegranate, *but for want of a better word . . .*

We are at the hands of mistaken men, *Bodies is another theme,* K said of her memoir

[the newspapers' headlines are screaming]

The wind is saying this landscape, this sea, this sky's Delacroix clouds, are yours

iv

On the lip of what was predicted
shopping daily for fruit and bread, and other things too

the cicadas kept their monotone chant
the sun was there and the sea's azures

when we let ourselves
read the headlines the azures and cicadas

helped travel us beyond the headlines, this was also true for

K, and the other students

who had brought their work to workshop

I want to take some of the weight of your ruin with me, K said

& I wanted to say grief is a location, forcing
location: you live in specificities & repetitions
. . . *red on red on red.* Kutta, *the man / in khaki says.*

v

The scent of the woman in line at the ATM is overwhelming
my skin feels peeled
(*If I were like you. If you were like me.*
Did we not stand
under one trade wind?
We are strangers.)

[notice all the frozen meat in a shopping cart]
K keeps seeing her mother

raped—having left the mall on an errand to exchange
a piece of clothing that didn't fit
two men abducted her in the parking lot—

Grief will keep you reaching back
for what is not there

I understand, I smiled, I understand it is important
to make overtures

vi

Try to be gentle when you feel the least able
[so I did laundry, picked up clothes that were on chairs & the bed & folded them
I was almost tender hanging out his underwear]
Try to be gentle when you feel you have been emptied—
[I filled the refrigerator, bought extra milk]

Grief keeps you open. K keeps imagining
the rape
to save what cannot be saved

I hug and thank her for buying dinner

She takes what she remembers—it's important
to find the repetitions—*Mother's feet. Bayonets. Teeth*

Map a way

In one of the interviews with a *Birangona*, a *war heroine*, the name the Bangladeshi
state gave to *the two hundred thousand women raped during the War of Independence*

Faizullah writes—
"Was it on a jute mat that
she gave birth to the baby
half-his or his or his? *Victim
a living being sacrificed.*"
You gather what's made you
otherwise,
more than the words you keep

losing—

lizards, sea shawl, impossible

You will be changed anyway—
I was on an island
it felt so much bigger than me
I gathered what we each wrote
very seriously, and found my repetitions—

lover, Europe, grief

NOTES

Passage on pg. 7 from Odysseus Elytis, *Journal of an Unseen April*, translated by David Connolly (Ypsilon Books, 1998).

Passage on pg. 15 from Tomas Tranströmer, *Selected Poems 1954–1986*, Ed. Robert Hass, translated by Robert Bly (Ecco Press, 1987).

"The Evening the Referendum Was Repealed" refers to the November 3, 2011 decision of the George Papandreou government to repeal the referendum that had been announced on November 1.

"Hemorrhaging Map" is for Eleni Stamopoulou, who provided the repeated line.

"The Taxi Driver Laments" makes unnamed reference to George Papandreou, the Minister of Education (1988–1989; 1994–1996) during the Panhellenic Socialist Party (PASOK) government under his father, Andreas Papandreou; GP also served as Prime Minister (2009–2011).

"This City" uses a quoted line from A. E. Stallings' translation of C. P. Cavafy's "The City" in *HAPAX*.

"Erasures" references "Mavros Kleitos" (c. 374 BC–328 BC) or "Black Kleitos," an officer of the Macedonian army led by Alexander the Great. Although he saved Alexander's life in the battle of Granicus, Alexander killed him some months later during a drunken fight when Kleitos criticized Alexander's treatment of his soldiers.

"Fatherland" uses the word *patrida* or πατρίδα (Greek for country, birthplace) for its connotations, too, of *patria* or πατριά (i.e. lineage, family); and *laiki* (Greek for the outdoor vegetable and fruit market). "Indignants," or the "Indignant Citizen's Movement" (Κίνημα Αγανακτισμένων Πολιτών) were activists who occupied Syntagma Square the summer of 2010 to protest the terms of the first bailout loans.

"Promise" references the early days of the SYRIZA government elected January 26, 2015 on an "anti-bailout" and "anti-austerity" platform in Greece.

"Reading with Ethel" is for Ethel Rackin.

Passage on pg. 37 from Italo Calvino, "Lightness," from *Six Memos for the Next Millennium* (Vintage International, 1988).

"Clothing the Dead" is for Amalia Melis.

"Winter, Why?" is for Jason Psaropoulos.

"Because Happiness is Temporary, Uncertain, & Hospitable" is for Deborah Reed.

"Kinds of Places" is for Joseph Powell.

"The Wound, a Mouth, an Eye" uses a line from Carolyn Forché's "Because One Is Always Forgotten" from *The Country Between Us* as its epigram. The poem also uses a line by the Greek poet Katerina Iliopoulou, who said, "A wound is also an eye."

Monica Sok, "Nocturne" from http://aaww.org/locked-eyes-monica-sok/

"Where the Contour Lies" is influenced by Sylvia Plath's "Daddy"; the repeated line "*Stranger-man, stranger-man . . .* " echoes Plath's "Panzer-man, panzer-man, O You—".

"Plateia Mavili" uses a line from David Lazar's poem "Ballad of a Narrative" from *Powder Town* as its epigram.

"The Goodbyes" is for Christina Kkona. The poem uses Yeats' line from his epitaph: "Cast a cold eye / On life, on death. / Horseman, pass by!" which concludes "Under Ben Bulben."

"Sea" is in memory of Michael Fakinos, 1954–2010.

"Poem in Pieces, a Log" uses quoted lines from Tarfia Faizullah's *Seam* (Southern Illinois University Press, 2014), and Paul Celan's "Language Mesh" translated by Michael Hamburger (POETRY, 1971).

BIOGRAPHICAL NOTE

Adrianne Kalfopoulou lives and teaches in Athens, Greece, where she heads the English and Modern Languages Department at Deree College and is a faculty mentor for the Mile High low-residency MFA Program at Regis University. Her publications include two collections of poetry, *Wild Greens* (2002), a finalist for the Benjamin Saltman award, and *Passion Maps* (2009), and a collection of essays, *Ruin: Essays in Exilic Living* (2014), all from Red Hen Press. Poems, essays, blog posts, and assemblages have appeared in journals, chapbook presses, and anthologies including *The Harvard Review online, Slag Glass City, Hotel Amerika, Superstition Review*, Dancing Girl Press, *Futures: Poetry of the Greek Crisis*, and *Borderlands and Crossroads: Writing the Motherland*.